ANIMALS IN THE WILD

RED PANDA

Annette Whipple

A Crabtree Forest Book

Crabtree Publishing
crabtreebooks.com

Notes for Readers and Class Discussion

This book is designed to teach readers about core subject areas, build curiosity, and inspire further investigation. Readers are encouraged to build upon what they already know about the subject and engage in topics they want to learn more about. Here are a few guiding questions to prompt reflection and discussion. Possible answers appear in red.

Before Reading:

Read the title and look at the table of contents. What do you already know about red pandas?

- *I know that red pandas have bushy tails.*
- *I know that red pandas in the wild live in forests.*

What would you like to learn about red pandas?

- *I would like to learn about what the red panda eats.*
- *I would like to learn whether the red panda is endangered.*

During Reading:

Pause after reading each page or chapter. What questions do you have about what you read? What are you curious to know?

- *I wonder why the two red panda subspecies evolved differently over time.*
- *I am curious to know why red pandas live in high elevations.*

Make connections to what you are reading. How is this like something you already know?

- *I know that some animals, such as foxes, use their bushy tails for warmth in cold weather.*
- *I know that climate change is a threat to the habitats of many animals.*

After Reading:

Recall key details about the book. What was the author trying to teach readers?

- *The author was trying to teach readers about the characteristics, behaviors, and habitats of red pandas.*
- *The author was trying to teach readers about what is being done to try to keep red pandas from becoming extinct.*

How did the images and captions help you understand more?

- *The photographs helped to show me what the red panda looks like in its habitat.*
- *The captions helped me understand new details about red pandas.*

Table of Contents

Meet the Red Panda

What ring-tailed animal with rust-colored fur lives in Asia? The red panda! This small mammal is about the size of a house cat. Red pandas are related to raccoons and weasels and are known for their cuteness.

The red panda's name is believed to have come from the Nepali words *nigalya ponya*, meaning "**bamboo-footed.**" Nepali is the most widely spoken language of Nepal—one of the mountain countries where red pandas live.

Lesser Is More

Red pandas are known scientifically as lesser pandas. There are two **subspecies**: the Himalayan red panda and the Chinese red panda. They shared the same **ancestors** millions of years ago, but **evolved** differently over time.

Not Related

Scientists named the red panda in the early 1800s. This was about 50 years before the giant panda was named. Despite their common "panda" name, the red panda and the giant panda are not related. Red pandas are also not as widely known as giant pandas. Red pandas have several different names, including lesser pandas, red cat-bears, and fire foxes.

Chapter 1

What Do They Look Like?

Red pandas are not really "red." They have thick, rust-colored fur that covers most of their bodies. They also have distinct white markings on their noses, above their eyes, and on the sides of their heads.

Red pandas have triangular ears with white fur inside them. They also have long, stiff whiskers around their mouths that they use to sense the environment.

Mammals

Red pandas are mammals. All mammals share some of the same characteristics. They keep a constant body temperature even as their environment gets warmer or colder. Hair or fur covers their skin. Females give birth to live young and feed their young with the milk the mother produces.

Red Coat Camo

The rusty coats of red pandas are believed to be **camouflage**. Their natural **habitat** is in the mixed mountain forests of Asia. Their coats, brown bushy tails with ring patterns, and brown-and-white faces help them hide among the red moss and white lichen-covered trees of their wild habitat.

Lichen is a slow-growing organism that can be found on a variety of surfaces, including trees, rocks, and soil.

Red pandas' tails are striped and incredibly bushy. Their tails help them balance on tree branches. They also curl their tails around their bodies to stay warm in the winter.

Long Tail

Red pandas have bearlike bodies, but they are much smaller than bears. They weigh 8 to 14 pounds (4–6 kg). Their bodies measure about 2 feet (61 cm) long, and their fluffy tails stretch to about 1.5 feet (46 cm)—nearly as long as their bodies! They have small heads and snouts. The Himalayan red panda is a little smaller than the Chinese red panda.

Claws on Show

Red pandas' claws are semi-retractable, which means the claws don't fully tuck inside their paws. They always show a little bit. They use their sharp claws while climbing trees and in self-defense. They don't use their claws to **forage** for food. Instead red pandas use their paws to grab and grasp bamboo.

Red pandas have strong skulls and jaw muscles, which help them chew tough bamboo.

Impawsible Thumb

A red panda's front paws look like they have thumbs, but they aren't really thumbs. These "false thumbs" are actually part of the wrist bone. They allow red pandas to flexibly climb and grip food. Giant pandas, who are also bamboo-eaters, have this false thumb too. **Fossil** evidence shows they each developed this **adaptation** for different reasons. The red panda's evolved mainly for climbing, although it also uses its false thumbs to eat.

Ancient Ancestors

There has been much debate over what animals were the ancient ancestors of red pandas. Scientists have been studying red panda **DNA** since the mid-1990s. Each new discovery furthered their belief that red pandas are the only living members of the Ailuridae family. All the other members are now **extinct**. The Ailuridae family is part of a "super family" of related animals which includes weasels and skunks. The red panda diverged, or took a different evolutionary path, from its closest relatives 40 million years ago.

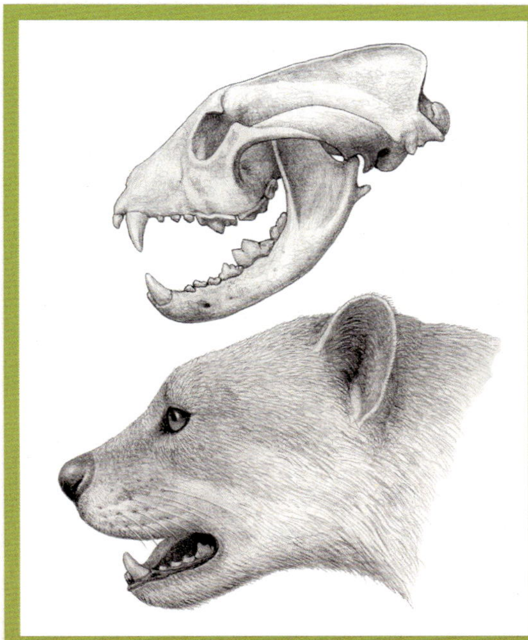

The simocyon, a prehistoric relative of the red panda, was a **carnivore** with a false thumb that could climb trees. It lived about 5 million years ago.

weasel

Chapter 2

Home and Habitat

Red pandas live in high **elevations** in many countries in Asia. Most live in China, but they are also found in Nepal, India, Bhutan, Myanmar, and beyond.

Forest Dwellers

Red pandas are found in the forests of high mountains such as the Himalayas. They climb trees and move from branch to branch and tree to tree. Red pandas prefer areas with lots of dense bamboo and shrubs.

Where Exactly?

The red panda's habitat includes the South Asian country of Nepal, where they live in the subalpine forests of the Himalayan mountain range. Their other habitats include India's states of Sikkim, West Bengal, and Arunachal Pradesh. Red pandas also live in Bhutan, Myanmar, and southern Tibet. The largest population of red pandas is found in China—about half of all red pandas in the wild are found in the Chinese provinces of Sichuan and Yunnan.

Some red pandas live in protected habitats in the eastern Himalayan broadleaf forests of Nepal, India, Bhutan, and China. These areas include evergreen and deciduous trees.

At Home

The habitats where red pandas live have average temperatures of 50 to 77 °Fahrenheit (10–25 °C). When cold weather arrives, red pandas do not **hibernate**. Instead, they go **dormant**, only waking up occasionally to eat. They barely move at all so that they can use their energy to stay warm. A red panda's thick fur coat and tail help keep it at a constant temperature.

Coniferous forests are dominated by evergreen trees such as pines, spruce, and fir. Broadleaf forests are dominated by trees that lose their leaves in autumn.

Red pandas define their territory through **scent marking**. Though these animals prefer to be by themselves, their home ranges overlap with other red pandas.

Defining Ranges

Red pandas inhabit forests that are from 7,900 to 12,800 feet (2,400 to 3,900 m) in elevation, preferring areas with bamboo understories. Each red panda tends to inhabit a small range, but they're always close to water. They spend most of their time in trees. Although they prefer broadleaf forests, they also live in evergreen, coniferous, deciduous, and mixed forests.

Total Habitat

Biologists who study red pandas estimate the total "potential" habitat—or the amount of suitable land they could possibly live on—is about 54,000 square miles (140,000 sq. km). Most of this habitat is in China and India. However, the animals only live on about 22,400 square miles (58,000 sq. km) because their habitat has been taken over by human development.

Fragmented Forest

Most wild red pandas live in forest fragments, or pieces of land that may not be connected. One species, *Ailurus fulgens fulgens*, lives mainly in Nepal, Bhutan, India, and western China. The other species, *Ailurus fulgens stytani*, is commonly found in China and Myanmar.

Fragmented forests make it more difficult for red pandas to travel to find food and potential mates.

Chapter 3

What to Eat?

A tall, leafy grass called bamboo makes up 95 percent of the red panda's diet. One red panda eats about 20,000 bamboo leaves in a single day and spends about half of the day grazing.

Time to Eat

A hungry red panda pulls a stalk of bamboo toward itself with its paws. It brings the bamboo to its mouth. The red panda bites off a single leaf. Then it chews and swallows. The red panda usually eats lower leaves on a stalk of bamboo. When bamboo leaves are out of reach, the red panda walks on fallen logs and shrubs and stretches for higher leaves.

Red pandas spend half their days eating bamboo shoots and leaves. They prefer early growth bamboo and fruit. These are tender and easy to digest, but only available in spring.

Other animals, such as the giant panda, also eat bamboo. However, red pandas and giant pandas don't compete for the same bamboo since they are usually in different forests.

Digestive System

Although red pandas rarely eat meat, their **digestive system** is that of a carnivore. Carnivores have short digestive systems, meaning food moves quickly through their bodies. It is hard for the red panda's digestive system to process bamboo and they must eat a lot of it to get the energy and nutrients they need.

Red pandas adapt to foods in different environments.

Sweet Tooth

In studying what red pandas eat, scientists have discovered that they have a sweet tooth. In one study, red pandas were offered a number of foods, including some that were artificially sweetened. They preferred the sweetened foods. Scientists believe this is why red pandas in the wild love ripe fruits—because they are usually sweet.

Checking Poo

Wildlife biologists examine the droppings of red pandas to understand what they eat and how much they eat. During winter months, red pandas eat only bamboo. In other seasons, they also eat fruits and berries when they're available, as well as the occasional insect, bird egg, and small lizard. They even eat flower blossoms. Red pandas also drink from a water source at least once a day.

Chapter 4

Red Panda Behavior

Red pandas are solitary animals, preferring to be by themselves. However, they do occasionally spend time with other red pandas. They also sometimes travel in pairs and as families.

Look at Me!

Although typically loners, red pandas communicate with one another in a variety of ways. They tend to stare at one another from a distance. Every red panda has a unique forehead pattern which may help them recognize one another. They mainly communicate through sounds called vocalizations, as well as scent marking.

Red pandas inspect scents by using large papillae on the bottom tip of their tongues. Papillae are bumps that function as sensory organs.

Using Their Voice

Red pandas communicate through a variety of sounds and gestures. When fighting, red pandas growl, bark, and grunt. They squeal if attacked. When defending themselves, they arch their backs and puff intensely. They might shake their heads from side to side or raise and lower them. They also stand on their hind legs and swat at one another.

Scent Communicators

Red pandas use chemical smells called **pheromones** to communicate as well. Smells in pee and poop send different messages. Red pandas even leave scent marks with the soles of their feet. One red panda leaves a scent behind. Other red pandas sniff and lick marked surfaces such as trees and rocks. This is how they learn about the red panda who left the mark.

Tree Dwellers

Red pandas are natural climbers who spend little time on the ground. Using their tails for balance and flexible joints for **agility**, they spend most of their time in trees. When it's time to move to the ground, they always descend headfirst, gripping the tree trunk with their back claws.

The red panda's main natural **predators** are snow leopards and martens.

On the ground, red pandas walk similarly to bears. This is because they swing their front legs inward like bears.

Red pandas can be shy. They are rarely aggressive but will clap their jaws when irritated.

Grooming Habits

Red pandas groom, or clean themselves, frequently. They often start grooming after waking up and eating. Red pandas groom much like cats do. They use their tongues to clean themselves. They often pull their tails to their mouths to groom them.

Staying Warm

Since their habitat is often cold, and nutrition from bamboo is minimal, red pandas limit their activity. To conserve energy in cold weather, they rest in trees throughout the day. These naps often last for more than two hours at a time. They perk up to eat. To stay warm, red pandas curl their tails around themselves.

Known as "heat-sensitive" animals, red pandas prefer temperatures cooler than 77 °Fahrenheit (25 °C).

Chapter 5

The Next Generation

Red pandas also rely on pheromones to communicate about **mating**. These scent messages are how males and females introduce themselves to potential mates.

Courtship

During mating season, red pandas form small "courtship" groups. Mating couples may even play together. They lunge and wrestle. Females mark their territory with a scent. Males inspect markings with a sniff—and even with a lick. Their tongues examine scents much like noses do. Males also leave marks over the female's mark.

Red pandas continue to spend time together after mating.

Marking and Mating

After a scent message, the male and female red pandas meet and interact. They forage and feed together, rest together, and move around the forest together as they get to know one another before mating. The female invites the male to mate with a flick of her tail.

Making a Nest

Female red pandas are pregnant for about four and a half months. Pregnancy uses a lot of energy. During the last month or so the pregnant red panda is tired and sluggish. Then, several days before she gives birth, she gets a burst of energy. This is when she collects sticks, grass, leaves, bark, and moss to prepare a nest. Nests are located in trees, or in rock crevices in the forest understory.

Nests can be found anywhere a mother red panda finds a quiet, safe place for her newborn cubs.

At birth, a red panda weighs just 3.5 ounces (100 g), or as much as a medium-sized tomato.

Twins and Quads

Usually, two red panda cubs are born to a litter—but sometimes as many as four cubs are born. Cubs are born helpless, so the mother cleans her babies right away. Cubs are also blind at birth. The mother provides for all their needs. She protects the newborns and rarely leaves them. Cubs are covered in fluffy, silver hair, and their tiny tails have no rings. The rings appear as they grow and age.

No-Mess Mama

For the first few weeks, all the cubs do is sleep and drink their mother's milk. After two weeks, the cubs open their eyes. Around this time, their reddish fur begins to grow. The mother helps the cubs pee and poop. She also keeps the nest clean, including eating all of her cubs' waste, so that a predator is less likely to find them.

Male red pandas are known to help care for their young by bringing food to a nest. They also sometimes protect the nest.

When red pandas are about a year old, they look like an adult. It takes a few more months for them to fully mature. Red pandas in the wild can live for 10 years or more.

Moving Time

The mother red panda moves her family to a new nesting site several times during the first few weeks of the cubs' lives. She carries them in her mouth. Young red pandas begin to chew bamboo twigs their mother brings them when they're about two months old. Sometimes the mother chews bamboo leaves to feed her young cubs. Cubs eat bamboo regularly when they're about three months old, and stop drinking their mother's milk soon after.

Chapter 6

Red Panda Conservation

Scientists have declared red pandas an **endangered** species. That means they are at high risk of extinction in the wild based on the threats that they face. Red pandas are in serious trouble and need help.

Threats to Red Pandas

In the wild, snow leopards, martens, golden eagles, and other predators hunt red pandas. When they feel threatened, red pandas climb trees to safety. When the threat is close, red pandas strike with their claws. But wild animal predators are not the ones reducing the red panda population. Humans and human activities are by far the biggest threats to red panda survival—through **poaching**, accidental trapping, and habitat loss.

Some hunters set traps for musk deer but accidentally kill red pandas.

Some red pandas are captured as part of the illegal pet trade. Hunting red pandas is against the law, but some are still killed. Their **pelts** are sold for clothing and their bodies are sold for meat.

Hunting and Agriculture

Because they are an endangered species, national and international laws protect against hunting red pandas in China, Nepal, Bhutan, India, and Myanmar. But this doesn't stop the animals from being poached. Others die because of their proximity, or nearness, to humans. As agriculture spreads closer to red panda habitats, forests are made into grazing lands for livestock such as cattle. Red pandas have lost much of their habitat to **deforestation**. As human populations increase, forest land decreases due to expanding development.

Roads and Bridges

Forests are cut down for logging, firewood, and to make room for homes and infrastructure such as roads and bridges. Since bamboo grows in forests, red pandas lose more than their homes when their forest habitat is gone. They lose their primary food source, as well as their nesting sites. When habitats are separated from one another, red pandas may not be able to find mates.

When development forces red pandas out of their wild habitat, many cannot adapt to new territory and they don't survive. Those that do survive end up living in fragmented bits of forest.

Climate Change

In the wild, the red panda's forest habitat is threatened by **climate change**. Warming temperatures force them to move to forests at higher elevations to adapt. In many of these areas, red pandas compete with humans for forest space and trees. For example, in the northeastern Indian state of Sikkim, people rely on firewood for cooking. This means more forests are cut, resulting in less habitat for red pandas.

The World Wildlife Fund says 70 percent of red panda habitat in Sikkim is located outside of red panda protection areas.

Conservation Efforts

There are about 10,000 red pandas in the wild. Wildlife **conservation** organizations are trying to preserve the red panda's habitat and secure its future. Red Panda Network is one group that works to help save red pandas in the wild through education. They support the people who live in and near red panda habitats through training and education programs that help them participate in red panda conservation while also earning a living.

Humans must learn how to share land with animals for red pandas to survive.

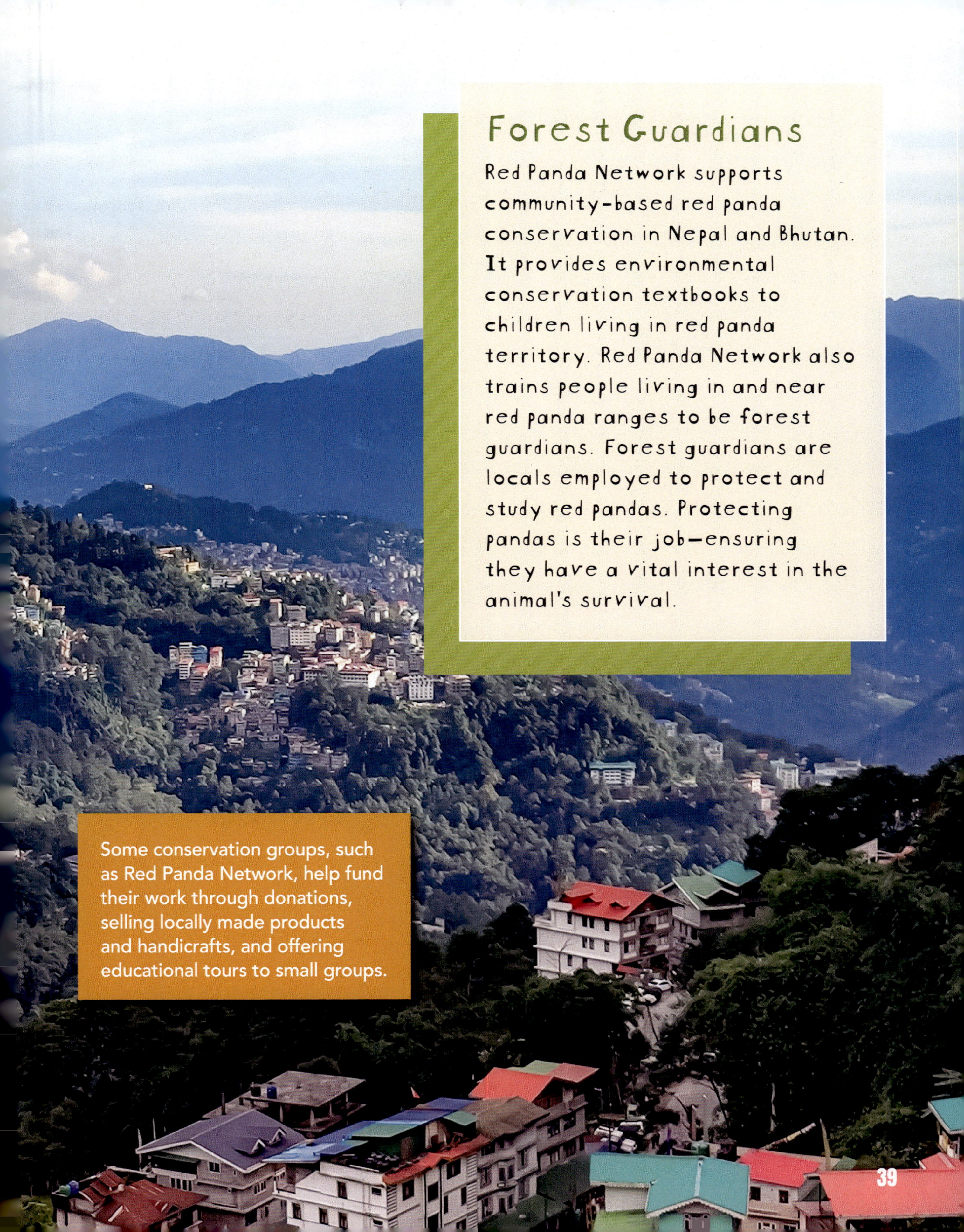

Forest Guardians

Red Panda Network supports community-based red panda conservation in Nepal and Bhutan. It provides environmental conservation textbooks to children living in red panda territory. Red Panda Network also trains people living in and near red panda ranges to be forest guardians. Forest guardians are locals employed to protect and study red pandas. Protecting pandas is their job—ensuring they have a vital interest in the animal's survival.

Some conservation groups, such as Red Panda Network, help fund their work through donations, selling locally made products and handicrafts, and offering educational tours to small groups.

Still Threatened

Red pandas were first declared an endangered species in 1988. Despite this, their population has shrunk 50 percent in the last 20 years. Red pandas are known as an umbrella species. Protecting their habitat protects the entire **ecosystem**. Biologists and conservationists know that educating and supporting the people living in or near the red panda's habitat helps the animal, as well as all other wild animals in the habitat.

Some red pandas live on preserves created to protect other animals such as giant pandas, but they still need help to protect against extinction.

Hope for the Future

Scientists evaluate many details to decide if an animal species needs help to survive. They look at:

- total population, and if the population is growing or decreasing
- natural habitat availability and how much is needed
- conservation efforts

Wolong National Nature Reserve is also home to about 150 giant pandas.

China's Plan

China has more than 30 wildlife protection areas within the red panda's range. This amounts to 6,120 square miles (15,846 sq. km) of protected territory. These areas include Gaoligongshan National Nature Reserve in Yunnan province, and Wolong National Nature Reserve in Sichuan province. The Chinese government has strict laws preventing the hunting, purchasing, and selling of red pandas.

Some Asian countries display the red panda on stamps and coins. Red pandas are also featured in movies, video games, and comic books around the world.

Zoo Conservation

Many zoos around the world help conserve wild animals through international agreements and programs. One such program is the Species Survival Plan (SSP), which protects animals at risk of extinction. Zoos throughout the world manage breeding programs. These help protect the **genetic diversity** of wild animals by sharing captive populations and not **inbreeding**.

Padmaja Naidu Himalayan Zoological Park in India has the world's most successful captive breeding program for red pandas. It started in 1994 with red pandas from the Cologne Zoo, Madrid Zoo, and Rotterdam Zoo. It is the only breeding program that is located within the red panda's natural territory.

adaptation (ad-uhp-TEY-shuhn): A change in an animal or plant that makes it better able to live in its habitat

agility (uh-JIL-i-tee): The ability to move quickly and easily

ancestors (AN-ses-ters): Animals in the past from which modern animals developed

bamboo (bam-BOO): A woody plant with a hollow stem that is in the grass family

camouflage (KAM-uh-flahzh): Colors and patterns that help an animal blend in with its natural surroundings

carnivore (KAHR-nuh-vawr): An animal that eats mainly meat

climate change (KLAHY-mit cheynj): The long-term change in Earth's usual climate

conservation (kon-ser-VEY-shuhn): The protection of animals, plants, and their habitats

deforestation (dee-fawr-uh-STEY-shuhn): The permanent clearing of forests or large areas of trees

digestive system (dahy-JES-tiv SIS-tuhm): The set of organs in the body, including the stomach and intestines, that turns food into energy and nutrients

DNA (dee-en-EY): A material inside the body's cells that carries all the genetic information about how a living thing will look and function

dormant (DAWR-muhnt): A state of inactivity or rest

ecosystem (EE-koh-sis-tuhm): A community of living and nonliving things in their environment

elevation (el-uh-VEY-shuhn): The height of a place, usually measured above or below sea level

endangered (en-DEYN-jerd): An animal or plant species that is considered to be at a very high risk of becoming extinct in the wild

evolved (ih-VOLVD): Changed gradually over a long period of time to survive better in an environment

extinct (ik-STINGKT): No longer existing

forage (FAWR-ij): To search for food

fossil (FOS-uhl): The preserved remains or traces of remains of an animal or plant that lived long ago

genetic diversity (juh-NET-ik dahy-VUR-si-tee): The range of different inherited traits within a species

habitat (HAB-i-tat): The place where an animal or plant naturally lives and grows

hibernate (HAHY-ber-neyt): To spend the winter in a deep, sleeplike state

inbreeding (IN-bree-ding): When closely related plants or animals produce offspring together

mating (MEY-ting): When a male and female animal join together for the purpose of producing offspring

pelt (pelt): The skin of a dead animal with its hair or fur still attached

pheromone (FER-uh-mohn): A chemical substance that an animal produces to communicate with other animals of the same species

poach (pohch): To catch or kill an animal illegally

predator (PRED-uh-ter): An animal that hunts other animals for food

scent marking (sent MAHR-king): A behavior by some animals in which they use scents produced by their bodies to communicate with other animals

subspecies (SUHB-spee-sheez): A smaller group of animals or plants within a species

INDEX

1. True or False:
Red pandas are related to giant pandas.

2. The red panda's "false thumb" is used mainly for __________.
   a. fighting
   b. climbing
   c. foraging

3. In the wild, red pandas live in __________.
   a. deserts
   b. grasslands
   c. forests

4. True or False:
A red panda eats about 20,000 bamboo leaves in a single day.

5. True or False:
Red pandas live in large groups called troops.

6. The __________ is a natural predator of the red panda.
   a. snow leopard
   b. polar bear
   c. crocodile

7. True or False:
The red panda is an endangered species.

8. Red pandas have lost much of their habitat due to __________.
   a. floods
   b. fires
   c. deforestation

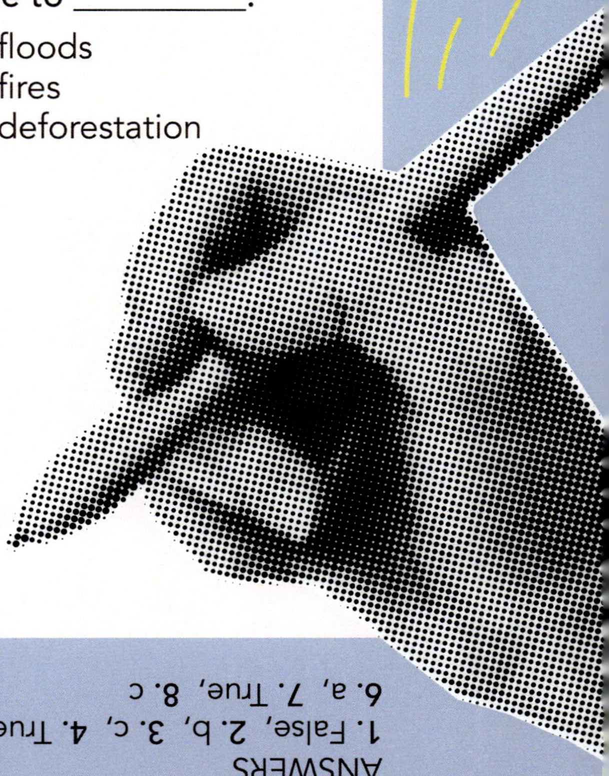

ANSWERS
1. False, 2. b, 3. c, 4. True, 5. False,
6. a, 7. True, 8. c

About the Author

Annette Whipple is the author of many children's books, including *The Laura Ingalls Wilder Companion: A Chapter-by-Chapter Guide, Whooo Knew? The Truth About Owls, and Quirky Critter Devotions: 52 Wild Wonders for Kids.* When Annette's not reading or writing, you might find her baking for her family in Pennsylvania. Get to know her at AnnetteWhipple.com.

Written by: Annette Whipple

Editor: Ellen Rodger

Proofreader: Melissa Boyce

Design and layout: Tammy McGarr

Production manager: Candice Campbell

Image Credits

Shutterstock: Tea Talk p 35, EricGr p 40, ANTONIOCR p 42 (bottom), zhuzhuxia, p 42 (top)

Wikimedia Commons: Creative Commons p 11 (top), p 13 (background & inset), p 31 (top), p 32, p 43 (bottom)

All other images from Shutterstock

Crabtree Publishing

crabtreebooks.com 800-387-7650

Hardcover 978-1-0398-7483-1
Paperback 978-1-0398-8437-3
Ebook (pdf) 978-1-0398-8196-9
Epub 978-1-0398-8316-1

Published in Canada
Crabtree Publishing
616 Welland Avenue
St. Catharines, Ontario
L2M 5V6

Published in the United States
Crabtree Publishing
347 Fifth Avenue
Suite 1402-145
New York, New York, 10016

Library and Archives Canada Cataloguing in Publication
Available at Library and Archives Canada

Library of Congress Cataloging-in-Publication Data
Available at the Library of Congress

Printed in the U.S.A./CP022026